Author: Jed Dolton
Publisher: Daoudi Publishing
ISBN: 978-1960809063

TABLE OF CONTENT

INTRODUCTION

This book is a valuable tool for young readers, specifically designed for second-grade students who are learning to read. It focuses on the important skill of decoding words and aims to help struggling readers improve their reading abilities at the word level. The book consists of 30 reading passages, each with comprehension questions to ensure that students understand what they have read.

The passages in the book use only decodable words, which means that they are made up of letters and letter combinations that students have already learned. This approach enables children to read independently and helps them gain confidence in their reading abilities.

The book follows a structured approach, teaching children the sounds that letters make (phonemes) in a specific order. It starts with the most commonly used phonemes and progresses to more complex ones. The activities included in each passage are designed to reinforce phonemic awareness and promote skill development, such as identifying sounds, tracing letters, filling in missing letters, and more.

Whether your child is a reluctant reader or struggling with reading, this book is a valuable resource for parents and teachers. It is convenient, easy to use, and provides an effective way to help young readers build a solid foundation in reading. With the help of this book, your child will be on their way to becoming a confident and proficient reader in no time.

THIS BOOK BELONG TO

_____

air

I CAN READ

Read the story, and identify and underline all the - air - words.

Red Birds and Butterfly Pins

Ava loved the fresh air of the countryside. One day, while walking, she saw a pair of red birds in the air. They were flying towards a fair. Lila followed and saw a big chair with a sign that said "hair salon." She decided to get her hair styled. The stylist gave her a braid with a hairpin that had a pair of butterflies. Lila was happy with her new hairdo and enjoyed the fair's sweet and savory treats while breathing in the fresh air

read and write

Write all the "air" words you can see in the story			

I CAN READ

Read the sentences and answers the questions: Put a check mark

Jack climbed the stair

Spider's hidden lair

Long curly hair

Questions

1. What did Jack climb?   train ☐   stair ☐

2. What was hidden in the lair?   spider ☐   cat ☐

Write the correct word beside each scrambled word.

hari	———	aiyr	———	stari	———
lari	———	laidr	———	scari	———
fari	———	bairn	———	mari	———

Make sentences

Lair _____

_____

Fair _____

_____

Trace it:

A I R   A I R   A I R

a i r   a i r   a i r

h a i r   h a i r   h a i r

Colour it:

3

I CAN WRITE

Color Me!

Circle the - air - words

bairn	mair	bleed
pow	deep	cairn
cheer	leaf	laird

Trace the words

mair   mair

pair   pair

fair   fair

Fill in the missing letters

fai _____   cair _____

hai _____   chai _____

mai _____   airt _____

Read and Trace the sentence.

The hair pair

The hair pair

READ AGAIN

Read the story, and answer each question. highlight the answers in the story.

Red Birds and Butterfly Pins

Ava loved the fresh air of the countryside. One day, while walking, she saw a pair of red birds in the air. They were flying towards a fair. Lila followed and saw a big chair with a sign that said "hair salon." She decided to get her hair styled. The stylist gave her a braid with a hairpin that had a pair of butterflies. Lila was happy with her new hairdo and enjoyed the fair's sweet and savory treats while breathing in the fresh air

Answer Each Question.

1 - What did Ava see while walking in the countryside?

_____

2 - What did Lila decide to do when she saw the sign for the hair salon?

_____

3 - What did Lila do while enjoying the sweet and savory treats at the fair?

_____

COLOR ME

Read and color the Letter

ank
I CAN READ

Read the story, and identify and underline all the - ank - words.

Prankster learns kindness

Hank the Tank loved to play pranks, but his friends weren't amused. They told him to stop or they'd leave him out of their games. Hank ankled away, feeling sad and alone. Later, he saw his friends playing without him and realized how much he missed them. He decided to apologize and promised never to prank them again. His friends forgave him and they all played together happily ever after. Hank learned that sometimes it's better to be kind than to be a prankster.

read and write

Write all the "ank" words you can see in the story			

I CAN READ

Read the sentences and answers the questions: Put a check mark

Hank played outside

He promised never to prank

His friends warned him, "Stop pranking!"

Questions

1. Where did Hank play?   outside ☐   inside ☐

2. What did promise never to do again?   prank ☐   play ☐

Write the correct word beside each scrambled word.

blakn	————	spakn	————	tankn	————
frakn	————	crakn	————	brakn	————
plakn	————	swakn	————	thakn	————

Make sentences

Thank
_____
- -
_____

Frank
_____
- -
_____

Rules
TRACE AND COLOR

Trace it:

ANK ANK ANK

and   and   and

thank   thank

I CAN WRITE

Color Me!

blank

Circle the - ank - words

blank	laud	flank
join	stank	pow
yanks	leaf	swank

Trace the words

plank plank
tank   tank
brank brank

Fill in the missing letters

bran _____   cran _____

blan _____   than _____

swan _____   bran _____

Read and Trace the sentence.

I have a tank

I have a tank

10

READ AGAIN

Read the story, and answer each question. highlight the answers in the story.

Prankster learns kindness

Hank the Tank loved to play pranks, but his friends weren't amused. They told him to stop or they'd leave him out of their games. Hank ankled away, feeling sad and alone. Later, he saw his friends playing without him and realized how much he missed them. He decided to apologize and promised never to prank them again. His friends forgave him and they all played together happily ever after. Hank learned that sometimes it's better to be kind than to be a prankster.

Answer Each Question.

1 - Why did Hank's friends tell him to stop playing pranks?

_____

2 - How did Hank feel when his friends left him out of their games?

_____

3 - What did Hank learn from his experience with his friends?

_____

COLOR ME

Read and color the Letter

ang

I CAN READ

Read the story, and identify and underline all the – ang – words.

Magical Feather Wings

Angie the Angel had a problem. She lost her wings and couldn't fly. Without her wings, she couldn't do her job of helping people. So, Angie went on a search to find her wings. She looked everywhere but couldn't find them. One day, she met a kind little girl who gave Angie a feather. The feather was magical and when Angie touched it, she grew new wings! Angie was so happy and grateful for the little girl's kindness. From that day on, Angie continued to help people with her new wings, and she never forgot the little girl who helped her.

read and write

Write all the "ang" words you can see in the story			

I CAN READ

Read the sentences and answers the questions: Put a check mark

Angela and her friend, love to play outside in the park.

The angry ants were marching

The angle of the sun was just right

Questions

1. Where does Angela love to play?   outside in the park ☐   in the car ☐

2. What were the angry ants doing?   play ☐   marching ☐

Write the correct word beside each scrambled word.

angle _____	angre _____	angsa _____
angre _____	angsa _____	angno _____
angts _____	angyl _____	angol _____

Make sentences

Anger _____
_____
_____

Angel _____
_____
_____

Rules
TRACE AND COLOR

Trace it:

ANG   ANG   ANG

ang   ang   ang

angel angel angel

Colour it:

I CAN WRITE

Color Me!

angst

Circle the - ang - words

blank	anglo	flank
angst	stank	cairn
angly	leaf	angas

Trace the words

angon angon
angly angly
angle angle

Fill in the missing letters

angl	___	angl	___
ange	___	anga	___
ange	___	angl	___

Read and Trace the sentence.

Loud bang

Loud bang

READ AGAIN

Read the story, and answer each question. highlight the answers in the story.

Magical Feather Wings

Angie the Angel had a problem. She lost her wings and couldn't fly. Without her wings, she couldn't do her job of helping people. So, Angie went on a search to find her wings. She looked everywhere but couldn't find them. One day, she met a kind little girl who gave Angie a feather. The feather was magical and when Angie touched it, she grew new wings! Angie was so happy and grateful for the little girl's kindness. From that day on, Angie continued to help people with her new wings, and she never forgot the little girl who helped her.

Answer Each Question.

1 - Who helped Angie find her wings?

_____

2 - What did the little girl give Angie?

_____

3 - What did Angie do after she got her new wings?

_____

COLOR ME

Read and color the Letter

ear

I CAN READ

Read the story, and identify and underline all the – ear – words.

Earl the Brave

Once upon a time, in a land far away, there was a little bear named Earl. Earl loved to explore the forest and play with his animal friends. One day, Earl heard a strange noise in the woods. It sounded like someone was crying. Earl followed the sound until he found a little rabbit who had hurt her ear. Earl knew just what to do. He gently cleaned and bandaged the rabbit's ear, and they became the best of friends. From that day on, Earl knew that listening for the sound of someone in need was the key to making new friends.

read and write

Write all the "ear" words you can see in the story			

I CAN READ

Read the sentences and answers the questions: Put a check mark

Jack learned to play guitar

We walked along the shoreline

Ava wears earrings every day

Questions

1. What does Jack do?   learned play guitar ☐   drive a car ☐

2. What does Ava wear?   play ☐   wears earrings ☐

Write the correct word beside each scrambled word.

heatr _____	pealr _____	earht _____
clera _____	early _____	leanr _____
yeanr _____	beadr _____	teasr _____

Make sentences

Heart
_____
_____

Clear
_____
_____

Rules
TRACE AND COLOR

Trace it:

EAR EAR EAR

ear ear ear ear

earth earth

Colour it:

 # I CAN WRITE

Color Me!

fear

Circle the - ear - words

fear	anglo	bear
angst	gear	cairn
near	leaf	angas

Trace the words

near   near
tear   tear
learn   learn

Fill in the missing letters

lear ____   pear ____

hear ____   eart ____

year ____   gea ____

Read and Trace the sentence.

I can hear you

i can hear you

READ AGAIN

Read the story, and answer each question. highlight the answers in the story.

Earl the Brave

Once upon a time, in a land far away, there was a little bear named Earl. Earl loved to explore the forest and play with his animal friends. One day, Earl heard a strange noise in the woods. It sounded like someone was crying. Earl followed the sound until he found a little rabbit who had hurt her ear. Earl knew just what to do. He gently cleaned and bandaged the rabbit's ear, and they became the best of friends. From that day on, Earl knew that listening for the sound of someone in need was the key to making new friends.

Answer Each Question.

1 - What did Earl learn about making friends?

_____

2 - What did Earl hear in the woods?

_____

3 - What did Earl like to do?

_____

COLOR ME

Read and color the Letter

eigh
I CAN READ

Read the story, and identify and underline all the - eigh - words.

Sledding with Eight and Pals

Leigh loved sledding with his friends eight, neigh, and weight. One winter day, they went to the top of a hill to sled down. The hill was steep and had a sharp curve at the bottom. leigh knew they had to be careful. They took turns sledding down, and everyone was having a blast. But then, it was Leigh's turn again, and he picked up too much speed. He started to panic as he approached the curve. But then, he remembered what his dad had told him: "If you feel scared, just close your eyes and scream!" So Leigh closed his eyes, screamed, and made it through the curve safely. His friends cheered, and Leigh felt proud of himself for being brave

read and write

Write all the "eigh" words you can see in the story			

25

I CAN READ

Read the sentences and answers the questions: Put a check mark

Eighteen is a multiple of nine

The sleigh ride was magical

We saw a rainbow tonight

(18)

Questions

1. What did you see after the rain stopped? dog ☐ rainbow ☐

2. What is eighteen divided by two? nine ☐ one ☐

Write the correct word beside each scrambled word.

weihg —— neihg —— reihg ——

eigth —— weigth —— veihg ——

heigth —— pligth —— neihg ——

Make sentences

Weigh _____

_____

Eight _____

_____

Rules
TRACE AND COLOR

Trace it:

EIGH   EIGH

eigh   eigh   eigh

weight   weight

Colour it:

I CAN WRITE

Color Me!

neigh

Circle the – eigh – words

weigh	anglo	height
neigh	gear	sleight
near	plight	angas

Trace the words

neigh   neigh
weigh   weigh
sleight sleight

Fill in the missing letters

eigh	——	freigh	——
weig	——	teig	——
neig	——	seig	——

Read and Trace the sentence.

The sleigh ride

The sleigh ride

READ AGAIN

Read the story, and answer each question. highlight the answers in the story.

Sledding with Eight and Pals

Leigh loved sledding with his friends eight, neigh, and weight. One winter day, they went to the top of a hill to sled down. The hill was steep and had a sharp curve at the bottom. leigh knew they had to be careful. They took turns sledding down, and everyone was having a blast. But then, it was Leigh's turn again, and he picked up too much speed. He started to panic as he approached the curve. But then, he remembered what his dad had told him: "If you feel scared, just close your eyes and scream!" So Leigh closed his eyes, screamed, and made it through the curve safely. His friends cheered, and Leigh felt proud of himself for being brave

Answer Each Question.

1 – What was at the bottom of the hill?

_____

2 – How did Leigh feel when he approached the curve?

_____

3 – How did Leigh feel after he made it through the curve?

_____

COLOR ME

Read and color the Letter

ew

I CAN READ

Read the story, and identify and underline all the - ew - words.

The Brave Little Ewok

Eddie the ewok was the smallest member of his tribe. He often felt left out because he was too small to help with important tasks like hunting and building. one day, while wandering through the forest, Eddie stumbled upon a group of lost baby birds. They were chirping loudly, calling for their mother who was nowhere to be found. eddie knew he had to help them, so he used his cleverness to create a makeshift nest out of twigs and leaves. He even found some berries for the birds to eat. the baby birds were so grateful that they chirped and sang all day long, keeping Eddie company and making him feel important. From that day on, Eddie knew that even the smallest creatures can make a big difference.

read and write

Write all the "ew" words you can see in the story			

I CAN READ

Read the sentences and answers the questions: Put a check mark

New ewe chewed blue gum

Drew few hewn screws

Queer brew grew anew

Questions

1. What did the new ewe chew?   blue gun ☐   run ☐

2. What happened to the queer brew?   two ☐   grew anew ☐

Write the correct word beside each scrambled word.

rene _____	sewe _____	skewe _____
crew _____	dewe _____	pewe _____
jewe _____	pewi _____	fewe _____

Make sentences

Renew

_____

_____

Jewel

_____

_____

32

Rules
TRACE AND COLOR

Trace it:

EW   EW   EW

ew   ew   ew

ewer   ewer

Colour it:

I CAN WRITE

Color Me!

pewit

Circle the - ew - words

pewit	screw	height
neigh	brews	sleight
near	plight	strew

Trace the words

strew strew
fewer fewer
jewel jewel

Fill in the missing letters

jewe ____   scre ____

crew ____   pewa ____

fewe ____   flew ____

Read and Trace the sentence.

Ewe blew

ewe blew

READ AGAIN

Read the story, and answer each question. highlight the answers in the story.

The Brave Little Ewok

Eddie the ewok was the smallest member of his tribe. He often felt left out because he was too small to help with important tasks like hunting and building. one day, while wandering through the forest, Eddie stumbled upon a group of lost baby birds. They were chirping loudly, calling for their mother who was nowhere to be found. eddie knew he had to help them, so he used his cleverness to create a makeshift nest out of twigs and leaves. He even found some berries for the birds to eat. the baby birds were so grateful that they chirped and sang all day long, keeping Eddie company and making him feel important. From that day on, Eddie knew that even the smallest creatures can make a big difference.

Answer Each Question.

1 - How did Eddie help the baby birds?

_____

2 - How did Eddie feel after helping the baby birds?

_____

3 - What is the importance of helping others?

_____

COLOR ME

Read and color the Letter

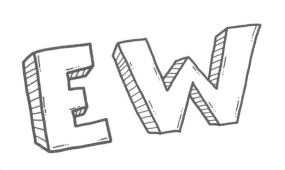

igh I CAN READ

Read the story, and identify and underline all the - igh - words.

Ingrid's Tree Climbing Adventure

Ingrid the iguana loved to climb trees. One day, she saw a juicy insect on a branch high up. Ingrid started to climb, but the branch was too thin, and she fell. "Ouch!" she cried. Ingrid felt sad and scared. She thought she could never climb again. But her friends, the other animals, gathered around her and said, "Don't worry, Ingrid! We'll help you." They taught her how to climb safely and cheered her on. Ingrid practiced every day and soon became the best tree climber in the jungle!

read and write

Write all the "igh" words you can see in the story			

I CAN READ

Read the sentences and answers the questions: Put a check mark

The bright light shone high

The kite flew in sight

The right shoe was too tight

Questions

1. How high did it shine? gun ☐ shone high ☐

2. How high did the kite fly? flew in sigh ☐ grew anew ☐

Write the correct word beside each scrambled word.

sigh _____   righ _____   high _____

ligh _____   migh _____   thig _____

nigh _____   tigh _____   figh _____

Make sentences

Light _____

_____

Night _____

_____

Rules
TRACE AND COLOR

Trace it:

IGH   IGH   IGH

igh   igh   igh

night   night

Colour it:

39

I CAN WRITE

Color Me!

sight

Circle the - igh - words

sight	light	height
neigh	night	fight
sleigh	plight	strew

Trace the words

fight   fight
sleigh   sleigh
right   right

Fill in the missing letters

sigh _____	figh _____
ligh _____	sleig _____
righ _____	right _____

Read and Trace the sentence.

The flight was quite

The flight was quite

READ AGAIN

Read the story, and answer each question. highlight the answers in the story.

Ingrid's Tree Climbing Adventure

Ingrid the iguana loved to climb trees. One day, she saw a juicy insect on a branch high up. Ingrid started to climb, but the branch was too thin, and she fell. "Ouch!" she cried. Ingrid felt sad and scared. She thought she could never climb again. But her friends, the other animals, gathered around her and said, "Don't worry, Ingrid! We'll help you." They taught her how to climb safely and cheered her on. Ingrid practiced every day and soon became the best tree climber in the jungle!

Answer Each Question.

1 - What did Ingrid the iguana love to do?

_____

2 - Why did Ingrid fall from the branch?

_____

3 - What did Ingrid do to become a better climber?

_____

COLOR ME

Read and color the Letter

ing
I CAN READ

Read the story, and identify and underline all the - ing- words.

The Flying Duckling

Once upon a time, there was a little duckling named Ping. Ping loved to swim in the pond with his siblings, but he always dreamed of flying high in the sky like the birds he saw above. One day, Ping saw a butterfly flitting around the flowers. Ping was fascinated by how effortlessly the butterfly flew, and he began practicing his own "flying" by flapping his wings as hard as he could. After many days of practice, Ping's wings grew strong enough for him to take flight. He soared above the pond, feeling the wind rushing through his feathers. From that day on, Ping was known as the Flying Duckling, and he lived happily ever after.

read and write

Write all the "ing" words you can see in the story			

I CAN READ

Read the sentences and answers the questions: Put a check mark

The dog is barking loudly

Birds are singing sweetly outside

Mom is cooking dinner now

Questions

1. What can you hear outside?   singing of birds ☐   noise ☐

2. What is Mom doing right now?   cooking dinner ☐   playing ☐

Write the correct word beside each scrambled word.

eatign ———	laughign ———	dancign ———
hikign ———	runnign ———	flyign ———
singign ———	bikign ———	playign ———

Make sentences

Playing _____

_____

Eating _____

_____

Rules
TRACE AND COLOR

Trace it:

ING ING ING

ing   ing   ing

flying   flying

Colour it:

I CAN WRITE

Color Me!

writing

Circle the – ing – words

sight	writing	height
running	night	fight
sleigh	playing	strew

Trace the words

biking biking
writing writing
flying flying

Fill in the missing letters

flyin _____ playin _____

hikin _____ readin _____

dancin _____ workin _____

Read and Trace the sentence.

I am jumping

i am jumping

46

READ AGAIN

Read the story, and answer each question. highlight the answers in the story.

The Flying Duckling

Once upon a time, there was a little duckling named Ping. Ping loved to swim in the pond with his siblings, but he always dreamed of flying high in the sky like the birds he saw above. One day, Ping saw a butterfly flitting around the flowers. Ping was fascinated by how effortlessly the butterfly flew, and he began practicing his own "flying" by flapping his wings as hard as he could. After many days of practice, Ping's wings grew strong enough for him to take flight. He soared above the pond, feeling the wind rushing through his feathers. From that day on, Ping was known as the Flying Duckling, and he lived happily ever after.

Answer Each Question.

1 – What did Ping dream of doing?

_____

2 – What inspired Ping to start flying?

_____

3 – What was Ping's nickname after flying?

_____

COLOR ME

Read and color the Letter

ink

I CAN READ

Read the story, and identify and underline all the - ink- words.

Pinky's Imaginative Writing Adventure

Once upon a time, there was a young girl named Pinky who loved to think of new ideas. She often sat at her desk, ink bottle in hand, and let her imagination run wild. One day, as Pinky was writing, she noticed a strange smell. It was coming from the sink, where a clog had caused the water to stink. Pinky tried to fix it, but it was no use. She needed help from her dad, who came to the brink of frustration before he finally fixed the problem. Afterward, they celebrated with a refreshing drink and a game of jinx, and Pinky went back to her writing, her mind still racing with new links and ideas.

read and write

Write all the "ink" words you can see in the story			

I CAN READ

Read the sentences and answers the questions: Put a check mark

Pink is my favorite color

Don't let your toy sink underwater

Be careful near the brink of the cliff

Questions

1.   What is your favorite color?   Pink   ☐   blue   ☐

2.   What to avoid with your toy?   sink underwater   ☐   go   ☐

Write the correct word beside each scrambled word.

thikn ———	sikn ———	stikn ———
wikn ———	brikn ———	shrikn ———
pikn ———	drikn ———	rikn ———

Make sentences

Think

_____

_____

Pink

_____

_____

Rules
TRACE AND COLOR

Trace it:

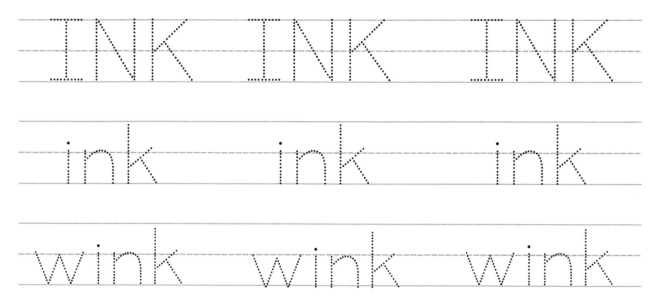

INK   INK   INK

ink   ink   ink

wink   wink   wink

Colour it:

WINK

I CAN WRITE

Color Me!

drink

Circle the - ink- words

drink	writing	link
running	blink	fight
sleigh	kink	stink

Trace the words

blink   blink
wink   wink
drink   drink

Fill in the missing letters

drin _____   stin _____

win _____   rink _____

brin _____   blin _____

Read and Trace the sentence.

Website Link

website link

READ AGAIN

Read the story, and answer each question. highlight the answers in the story.

Pinky's Imaginative Writing Adventure

Once upon a time, there was a young girl named Pinky who loved to think of new ideas. She often sat at her desk, ink bottle in hand, and let her imagination run wild. One day, as Pinky was writing, she noticed a strange smell. It was coming from the sink, where a clog had caused the water to stink. Pinky tried to fix it, but it was no use. She needed help from her dad, who came to the brink of frustration before he finally fixed the problem. Afterward, they celebrated with a refreshing drink and a game of jinx, and Pinky went back to her writing, her mind still racing with new links and ideas.

Answer Each Question.

1 - What did Pinky notice while writing?

_____

2 - Who did Pinky need help from to fix the problem?

_____

3 - What did Pinky love to do at her desk?

_____

COLOR ME

Read and color the Letter

ind
I CAN READ

Read the story, and identify and underline all the - ind- words.

Indy's Independent Adventure

Indy loved playing with her friends, but today she felt independent. She wanted to explore the woods alone. As she walked, she saw an indigenous bird with beautiful indigo feathers. It flew away before Indy could take a picture. Disappointed, she continued on her adventure. Suddenly, she heard an indistinct noise. She followed the sound until she found a tiny, injured hedgehog. Indy picked it up and took it home to her parents, who helped nurse it back to health.Indy realized that being independent didn't mean being alone, and that helping others was an important part of any adventure.

read and write

Write all the "ind" words you can see in the story			

I CAN READ

Read the sentences and answers the questions: Put a check mark

Today, she feels independent and free

Suddenly, she hears indistinct noise

A beautiful indigenous bird catches Ava's eye

Questions

1. She feels ?   independent ☐   angry ☐

2. indigenous bird catches?   catches Ava's eye ☐   playing ☐

Write the correct word beside each scrambled word.

indei _____   indir _____   indwo _____

indxe _____   indlo _____   indai _____

indeu _____   indce _____   indxo _____

Make sentences

India
_____
_____

Index
_____
_____

Rules
TRACE AND COLOR

Trace it:

IND IND IND

ind   ind   ind

indue indue indue

Colour it:

I CAN WRITE

Color Me!

indec

Circle the - ind- words

indec	writing	index
running	indri	fight
indol	indow	stink

Trace the words

indow indow

indie   indie

indue   indue

Fill in the missing letters

indu ____	indr ____
indo ____	inde ____
indo ____	indu ____

Read and Trace the sentence.

Indigenous Bird

indigenous bird

READ AGAIN

Read the story, and answer each question. highlight the answers in the story.

Indy's Independent Adventure

Indy loved playing with her friends, but today she felt independent. She wanted to explore the woods alone. As she walked, she saw an indigenous bird with beautiful indigo feathers. It flew away before Indy could take a picture. Disappointed, she continued on her adventure. Suddenly, she heard an indistinct noise. She followed the sound until she found a tiny, injured hedgehog. Indy picked it up and took it home to her parents, who helped nurse it back to health.Indy realized that being independent didn't mean being alone, and that helping others was an important part of any adventure.

Answer Each Question.

1 – Why did Indy feel independent today?

_____

2 – What did Indy see while exploring the woods?

_____

3 – What lesson did Indy learn on her adventure?

_____

COLOR ME

Read and color the Letter

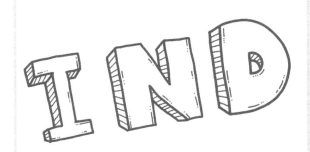

spl
I CAN READ

Read the story, and identify and underline all the - spl- words.

Puddle Friends Forever

Samantha loved splashing in puddles. She put on her rain boots and raincoat and headed outside. The rain was coming down hard, and the puddles were getting bigger. She splashed in one, then another, and another. Suddenly, she heard a strange splashing sound. She looked around and saw a little frog in a puddle. It was struggling to get out. Samantha reached in and scooped up the frog. She brought it inside and dried it off. From that day on, the little frog became Samantha's best friend. They loved splashing in puddles together, rain or shine.

read and write

Write all the "spl" words you can see in the story			

I CAN READ

Read the sentences and answers the questions: Put a check mark

The kids splash in puddles

She cried over the spilled milk

The dog loves to splash

Questions

1. What does the dog love?   splash ☐   running ☐

2. Who loves to splash?   dog ☐   bird ☐

Write the correct word beside each scrambled word.

splahs _____   splta _____   splitn _____

splti _____   splru _____   splien _____

splya _____   splasyh _____   spledn _____

Make sentences

Spill _____

_____

_____

Splay _____

_____

_____

Rules
TRACE AND COLOR

Trace it:

SPL SPL SPL

spl spl spl

split split split

Colour it:

I CAN WRITE

Color Me!

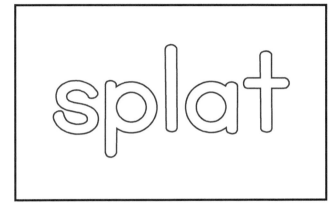

Circle the - spl - words

indec	spill	split
splay	indri	splat
indol	splur	stink

Trace the words

split split
spill spill
splat splat

Fill in the missing letters

spla _____	splin _____
splu _____	spla _____
splin _____	splas _____

Read and Trace the sentence.

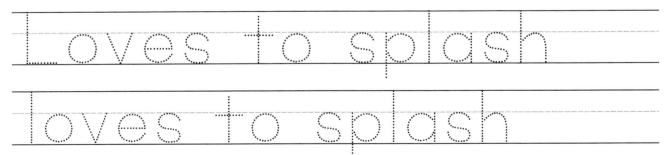

Loves to splash

loves to splash

READ AGAIN

Read the story, and answer each question. highlight the answers in the story.

Puddle Friends Forever

Samantha loved splashing in puddles. She put on her rain boots and raincoat and headed outside. The rain was coming down hard, and the puddles were getting bigger. She splashed in one, then another, and another. Suddenly, she heard a strange splashing sound. She looked around and saw a little frog in a puddle. It was struggling to get out. Samantha reached in and scooped up the frog. She brought it inside and dried it off. From that day on, the little frog became Samantha's best friend. They loved splashing in puddles together, rain or shine.

Answer Each Question.

1 - What did Samantha put on before heading outside?

_____

2 - What happened to the little frog after Samantha rescued it?

_____

3 - What did Samantha and the little frog enjoy doing together?

_____

COLOR ME

Read and color the Letter

str

I CAN READ

Read the story, and identify and underline all the – str – words.

Star Saves a Stray Dog

Sara loved to play with her toy stars. One day, she went to the park and saw a stray dog. It looked hungry and sad. Sara wanted to help, but she didn't know what to do. Suddenly, she had an idea! She ran home and grabbed some treats for the dog. When she returned, the stray dog was still there. Sara gave him the treats and the dog wagged its tail happily. Sara felt proud of herself for helping the stray dog, and she decided to name him "Star" because he had a little white star on his head.

read and write

Write all the "str" words you can see in the story			

I CAN READ

Read the sentences and answers the questions: Put a check mark

Stray cats often roam the streets

The strong wind blew my hat off

The string on my hoodie broke

Questions

1. Who roams the streets often?   cats ☐   dogs ☐

2. What blew your hat off?   rain ☐   strong wind ☐

Write the correct word beside each scrambled word.

strwa _____   strwe _____   stroeb _____

strtu _____   strpe _____   strpa _____

strpi _____   strya _____   strpo _____

Make sentences

Stress
_____
_____
_____

Strive
_____
_____
_____

Rules
TRACE AND
COLOR

Trace it:

STR STR STR

str str str

strip strip strip

Colour it:

I CAN WRITE

Color Me!

Circle the - str - words

indec	strum	strop
strive	indri	strong
indol	stray	stink

Trace the words

stray stray
stress stress
strive strive

Fill in the missing letters

striv _____   stra _____

stron _____   stru _____

stri _____   strea _____

Read and Trace the sentence.

The Strong Lion

the strong lion

READ AGAIN

Read the story, and answer each question. highlight the answers in the story.

Star Saves a Stray Dog

Sara loved to play with her toy stars. One day, she went to the park and saw a stray dog. It looked hungry and sad. Sara wanted to help, but she didn't know what to do. Suddenly, she had an idea! She ran home and grabbed some treats for the dog. When she returned, the stray dog was still there. Sara gave him the treats and the dog wagged its tail happily. Sara felt proud of herself for helping the stray dog, and she decided to name him "Star" because he had a little white star on his head.

Answer Each Question.

1 - What did Sara see at the park?

_____

2 - How did Sara feel when she saw the dog?

_____

3 - How did Sara feel after helping the dog?

_____

COLOR ME

Read and color the Letter

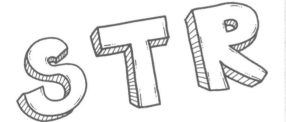

sion

I CAN READ

Read the story, and identify and underline all the - sion - words.

Collision of Worlds

Once upon a time, in a far-off land, a group of aliens arrived on Earth with a vision to create a new world. They asked for permission from the Earthlings to coexist peacefully. The Earthlings were hesitant but ultimately decided to allow the aliens to stay. unfortunately, a collision between the aliens and Earthlings caused an explosion, leading to widespread destruction. The Earthlings realized that their decision had caused harm and concluded that the aliens had to leave. The aliens were heartbroken and left Earth, which began to heal from the erosion caused by the explosion. The Earthlings learned the importance of precision in decision-making and the need for open-mindedness in revising their thinking.

read and write

Write all the "sion" words you can see in the story			

I CAN READ

Read the sentences and answers the questions: Put a check mark

Television provides visual entertainment

The precision of the machine was impressive

Revision can improve writing

Questions

1. What does television provide? reading ☐ entertainment ☐

2. What can improve writing? revision ☐ skills ☐

Write the correct word beside each scrambled word.

visino ————	divisino ————	abortino ————
fusino ————	televisino ————	collisino ————
missino ————	derisino ————	collisino ————

Make sentences

Vision
_____
_____
_____

Mission
_____
_____
_____

Rules
TRACE AND COLOR

Trace it:

SION   SION

sion   sion   sion

vision   vision

Colour it:

I CAN WRITE

Color Me!

fusion

Circle the - sion - words

indec   division   strop

fusion   indri   derision

indol   erosion   stink

Trace the words

division

precision

persuasion

Fill in the missing letters

collisio _____   visio _____

precisio _____   fusio _____

confusio _____   missio _____

Read and Trace the sentence.

Vision inspires us

vision inspires us

READ AGAIN

Read the story, and answer each question. highlight the answers in the story.

Collision of Worlds

Once upon a time, in a far-off land, a group of aliens arrived on Earth with a vision to create a new world. They asked for permission from the Earthlings to coexist peacefully. The Earthlings were hesitant but ultimately decided to allow the aliens to stay. unfortunately, a collision between the aliens and Earthlings caused an explosion, leading to widespread destruction. The Earthlings realized that their decision had caused harm and concluded that the aliens had to leave. The aliens were heartbroken and left Earth, which began to heal from the erosion caused by the explosion. The Earthlings learned the importance of precision in decision-making and the need for open-mindedness in revising their thinking.

Answer Each Question.

1 - Who arrived on Earth?

_____

2 - What did the aliens want to do on Earth?

_____

3 - What did Earthlings learn from the experience?

_____

COLOR ME

Read and color the Letter

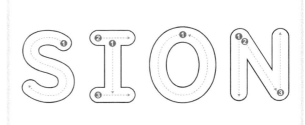

I CAN READ

Read the sentences and answers the questions: Put a check mark

Scrambled eggs taste amazing

The scrappy dog chased squirrels

Scribble on my notebook

Questions

1. What tastes amazing?   banana ☐   Scrambled eggs ☐

2. What did the scrappy dog do?   run ☐   chased squirrels ☐

Write the correct word beside each scrambled word.

scrbu _____   scrto _____   scrga _____

scrpa _____   scrdo _____   scrmu _____

scrim _____   scrvi _____   scrma _____

Make sentences

Scrub _____

_____

_____

Scrap _____

_____

_____

I CAN READ

Read the story, and identify and underline all the – scr – words.

Scramble at Shipyard

In the shipyard, workers scrambled to finish the ship. They realized they had used the wrong screws, so they searched for scriv specifications. The workers scoured the scrap pile and scrubbed the yard. Finally, they found the screws they needed and worked together in a scrum to fix the mistake. The ship set sail without any scrunching sounds. However, it hit a scrot of rocks, causing a screech. The workers sculped the broken parts in a scrum and fixed the ship. They learned to be more careful and avoid another scramble in the future.

read and write

Write all the "scr" words you can see in the story			

Rules
TRACE AND
COLOR

Trace it:

SCR SCR SCR

scr scr scr

scrap scrap

Colour it:

I CAN WRITE

Color Me!

scrun

Circle the - scr - words

scrun	division	strop
fusion	scrod	sculp
indol	screw	stink

Trace the words

screw screw
scrit scrit
scrag scrag

Fill in the missing letters

scra _____   scra _____

scri _____   scru _____

scro _____   scre _____

Read and Trace the sentence.

Scrub your hands

scrub your hands

READ AGAIN

Read the story, and answer each question. highlight the answers in the story.

Scramble at Shipyard

In the shipyard, workers scrambled to finish the ship. They realized they had used the wrong screws, so they searched for scriv specifications. The workers scoured the scrap pile and scrubbed the yard. Finally, they found the screws they needed and worked together in a scrum to fix the mistake. The ship set sail without any scrunching sounds. However, it hit a scrot of rocks, causing a screech. The workers sculped the broken parts in a scrum and fixed the ship. They learned to be more careful and avoid another scramble in the future.

Answer Each Question.

1 - What were the workers doing in the shipyard?

_____

2 - What did the workers do when they realized the mistake?

_____

3 - What did the workers do to fix the mistake?

_____

COLOR ME

Read and color the Letter

tion
I CAN READ

Read the story, and identify and underline all the – tion – words.

Rosie's Garden Transformation

A cute bunny named Rosie lived in a beautiful garden. One day, she noticed that the flowers were in a state of decay. Rosie decided to take action to fix the situation. She started to work on the garden by watering the plants, cleaning the area, and planting new flowers. She spent many hours to complete the job. The transformation was amazing, the garden was now full of vibrant colors and the flowers were in full bloom. Everyone in the garden was overjoyed and praised Rosie's determination. From that day on, Rosie became the official gardener and continued to work tirelessly to keep the garden in perfect condition.

read and write

Write all the "tion" words you can see in the story			

I CAN READ

Read the sentences and answers the questions: Put a check mark

The musician played beautiful compositions

The artist created stunning illustrations

The soldier received a commendation

Questions

1. What did the musician play?   football ☐   compositions ☐

2. What did the artist create?   illustrations ☐   car ☐

Write the correct word beside each scrambled word.

vacatino ———   fictino ———   directino ———

statino ———   emotino ———   motino ———

attentino ———   conditino ———   potino ———

Make sentences

Option

_____

_____

Action

_____

_____

Rules
TRACE AND COLOR

Trace it:

TION TION

tion tion tion

option option

Colour it:

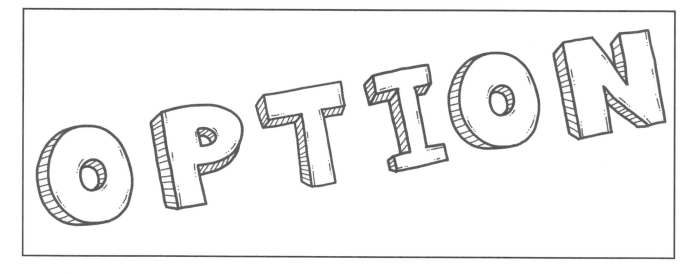

I CAN WRITE

Color Me!

potion

Circle the – tion – words

scrun	potion	strop
action	scrod	option
indol	motion	stink

Trace the words

option option

action action

potion potion

Fill in the missing letters

potio ____	potio ____
statio ____	optio ____
fictio ____	fusio ____

Read and Trace the sentence.

Deep concentration

deep concentration

READ AGAIN

Read the story, and answer each question. highlight the answers in the story.

Rosie's Garden Transformation

A cute bunny named Rosie lived in a beautiful garden. One day, she noticed that the flowers were in a state of decay. Rosie decided to take action to fix the situation. She started to work on the garden by watering the plants, cleaning the area, and planting new flowers. She spent many hours to complete the job. The transformation was amazing, the garden was now full of vibrant colors and the flowers were in full bloom. Everyone in the garden was overjoyed and praised Rosie's determination. From that day on, Rosie became the official gardener and continued to work tirelessly to keep the garden in perfect condition.

Answer Each Question.

1 - What did Rosie notice in the garden?

_____

2 - What did Rosie do to fix the situation?

_____

3 - How did the garden look after Rosie's work?

_____

COLOR ME

Read and color the Letter

ture

I CAN READ

Read the story, and identify and underline all the - ture - words.

Timmy's Nature Adventure

Timmy was fascinated with nature, literature, and different cultures. His parents surprised him with an adventure trip to a nearby forest, and he couldn't wait to explore. Timmy noticed the creatures, miniature plants, and beautiful scenery during their journey. He learned to nurture and maintain the environment's structure and even helped gather manure to help plants grow. After the trip, Timmy felt mature and responsible. He wanted to protect nature and its creatures, leaving his signature on the world. Timmy stood tall with proper posture, proud of his love for nature and culture. Looking at his picture, Timmy smiled, knowing his future was bright with endless possibilities.

read and write

Write all the "ture" words you can see in the story			

I CAN READ

Read the sentences and answers the questions: Put a check mark

The mature tree provided shade

The furniture was elegant and stylish

The structure of the building was impressive

Questions

1. What did the mature tree provide?   shade ☐   water ☐

2. What was the furniture like?   good ☐   elegant and stylish ☐

Write the correct word beside each scrambled word.

natuer ———   matuer ———   creatuer ———

futuer ———   postuer ———   lecturre ———

cultuer ———   pictuer ———   featuer ———

Make sentences

Nature
_____
- -
_____

Future
_____
- -
_____

Rules
TRACE AND
COLOR

Trace it:

TURE TURE

ture ture ture

culture culture

Colour it:

 # I CAN WRITE

Color Me!

mature

Circle the – ture – words

scrun	mature	strop
posture	scrod	picture
torture	motion	suture

Trace the words

suture

future

adventure

Fill in the missing letters

pictur .... lectur ....

creatur .... nurtur ....

lecture .... lectur ....

Read and Trace the sentence.

Informative lecture

informative lecture

READ AGAIN

Read the story, and answer each question. highlight the answers in the story.

Timmy's Nature Adventure

Timmy was fascinated with nature, literature, and different cultures. His parents surprised him with an adventure trip to a nearby forest, and he couldn't wait to explore. Timmy noticed the creatures, miniature plants, and beautiful scenery during their journey. He learned to nurture and maintain the environment's structure and even helped gather manure to help plants grow. After the trip, Timmy felt mature and responsible. He wanted to protect nature and its creatures, leaving his signature on the world. Timmy stood tall with proper posture, proud of his love for nature and culture. Looking at his picture, Timmy smiled, knowing his future was bright with endless possibilities.

Answer Each Question.

1 - Who surprised Timmy with an adventure trip?

_____

2 - What did Timmy notice during the journey?

_____

3 - How did Timmy feel after the trip?

_____

COLOR ME

Read and color the Letter

tch
I CAN READ

Read the story, and identify and underline all the - tch - words.

The Magic Sketchbook

Once there was a Dutch boy named Butch who loved to sketch and watch the stars at night with his telescope. One evening, while stargazing, he noticed a scotch-colored comet with a notch in its tail. Excited to catch it, he used a crutch to stretch and reach for his matchbox. But when he struck a match, the light scared away the comet. Disappointed, he went inside to fetch a flashlight and a map to teach himself how to navigate the night sky. From then on, Butch always kept his torch nearby for stargazing adventures.

read and write

Write all the "tch" words you can see in the story			

I CAN READ

Read the sentences and answers the questions: Put a check mark

The eggs are about to hatch any moment now

Ava's watch stopped ticking last night

I love the soft touch of my cat's fur

Questions

1. What is about to hatch?   the eggs ☐   tree ☐

2. Whose watch stopped ticking last night?   jack ☐   ava ☐

Write the correct word beside each scrambled word.

cathc ———   mathc ———   skethc ———

bathc ———   pathc ———   swithc ———

hathc ———   scrathc ———   beahc ———

Make sentences

Match _____

_____

_____

Switch _____

_____

_____

Rules

TRACE AND COLOR

Trace it:

TCH   TCH

tch   tch   tch

hatch   hatch

Colour it:

I CAN WRITE

Color Me!

match

Circle the - tch - words

match	potion	patch
action	scratch	option
batch	motion	switch

Trace the words

batch batch
hatch hatch
switch switch

Fill in the missing letters

catc _____   patc _____

batc _____   sketc _____

hatc _____   switc _____

Read and Trace the sentence.

The sketch pad

The sketch pad

READ AGAIN

Read the story, and answer each question. highlight the answers in the story.

The Magic Sketchbook

Once there was a Dutch boy named Butch who loved to sketch and watch the stars at night with his telescope. One evening, while stargazing, he noticed a scotch-colored comet with a notch in its tail. Excited to catch it, he used a crutch to stretch and reach for his matchbox. But when he struck a match, the light scared away the comet. Disappointed, he went inside to fetch a flashlight and a map to teach himself how to navigate the night sky. From then on, Butch always kept his torch nearby for stargazing adventures.

Answer Each Question.

1 - What did Butch notice while stargazing one evening?

_____

2 - How did Butch try to catch the comet?

_____

3 - What did Butch do to teach himself how to navigate the night sky?

_____

COLOR ME

Read and color the Letter

tch

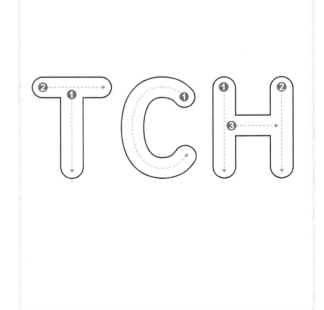

ong
I CAN READ

Read the story, and identify and underline all the - ong - words.

Musical Park Walk

Mia and her dog Pongo loved to take long walks in the park. One day, while they were walking, they heard a beautiful song. It was coming from a group of birds sitting on a tree branch. Mia and Pongo listened as the birds sang their song with perfect harmony. Mia was so inspired by the birds' song that she started singing along. Pongo barked happily, and soon they were all making music together. The birds sang, Mia hummed, and Pongo barked along to the beat. When they finished, Mia thanked the birds for the lovely serenade. The birds thanked Mia and Pongo for joining in and making their song even better. Mia and Pongo continued their walk, feeling grateful for the beautiful music they had shared with their feathered friends.

read and write

Write all the "ong" words you can see in the story			

I CAN READ

Read the sentences and answers the questions: Put a check mark

The project is still ongoing

The dancers moved to the conga beat

He was strong enough to lift the box

Questions

1. Is the project completed or ongoing?   completed ☐   ongoing ☐

2. What kind of music did the dancers move to?   play ☐ the conga ☐

Write the correct word beside each scrambled word.

sogn _____   alogn _____   thogn _____

logn _____   bogn _____   shogn _____

strogn _____   wrogn _____   oblogn _____

Make sentences

Song _____

_____

_____

Strong _____

_____

_____

Rules
TRACE AND COLOR

Trace it:

ONG   ONG

ong   ong   ong

long   long

Colour it:

I CAN WRITE

Color Me!

Circle the – ong – words

along	strong	patch
action	scratch	bong
wrong	tongue	switch

Trace the words

wrong wrong

long   long

bong   bong

Fill in the missing letters

son _____	thon _____
stron _____	oblon _____
wron _____	bon _____

Read and Trace the sentence.

I played ping pong

i played ping pong

READ AGAIN

Read the story, and answer each question. highlight the answers in the story.

Musical Park Walk

Mia and her dog Pongo loved to take long walks in the park. One day, while they were walking, they heard a beautiful song. It was coming from a group of birds sitting on a tree branch. Mia and Pongo listened as the birds sang their song with perfect harmony. Mia was so inspired by the birds' song that she started singing along. Pongo barked happily, and soon they were all making music together. The birds sang, Mia hummed, and Pongo barked along to the beat. When they finished, Mia thanked the birds for the lovely serenade. The birds thanked Mia and Pongo for joining in and making their song even better. Mia and Pongo continued their walk, feeling grateful for the beautiful music they had shared with their feathered friends.

Answer Each Question.

1 - Who enjoyed taking long walks in the park?

_____

2 - What did Mia and Pongo hear while they were walking?

_____

3 - How did Pongo react when Mia started singing?

_____

COLOR ME

Read and color the Letter

old

I CAN READ

Read the story, and identify and underline all the - old - words.

Bold Adventure Begins

Tessa was a bold girl who lived in an old-fashioned household. She set off on an adventure to find the threshold of a magical portal. As she walked, she came across an old man holding a scolding hot teapot in his moldy old house. She helped him, and he told her the location of the portal. Tessa continued her journey, crossed rivers, and climbed hills until she beheld the magnificent sight. She learned that helping others emboldened her. She returned home and told her family. They were proud of her for upholding kindness and courage. Tessa lived by the motto, "Hold onto your courage and always be bold."

read and write

Write all the "old" words you can see in the story			

I CAN READ

Read the sentences and answers the questions: Put a check mark

The book had an olden cover

The building had an old-fashioned look

The song had an old-timey feel

Questions

1. What did the book have on its cover? olden cover ☐ fresh ☐

2. What kind of look did the building have? old-fashioned look ☐ good ☐

Write the correct word beside each scrambled word.

oldne ————	molyd ————	codl ————
bodl ————	hodl ————	todl ————
moldre ————	fodl ————	sodl ————

Make sentences

Sold

Told

Rules
TRACE AND COLOR

Trace it:

OLD OLD

old old old

bold bold

Colour it:

I CAN WRITE

Color Me!

bold

Circle the - old - words

along	bold	patch
action	molder	fold
cold	tongue	switch

Trace the words

cold   cold
told   told
hold   hold

Fill in the missing letters

hol ____   sol ____

molde ____   scol ____

bol ____   olde ____

Read and Trace the sentence.

Olden times

olden times

READ AGAIN

Read the story, and answer each question. highlight the answers in the story.

Bold Adventure Begins

Tessa was a bold girl who lived in an old-fashioned household. She set off on an adventure to find the threshold of a magical portal. As she walked, she came across an old man holding a scolding hot teapot in his moldy old house. She helped him, and he told her the location of the portal. Tessa continued her journey, crossed rivers, and climbed hills until she beheld the magnificent sight. She learned that helping others emboldened her. She returned home and told her family. They were proud of her for upholding kindness and courage. Tessa lived by the motto, "Hold onto your courage and always be bold."

Answer Each Question.

1 - Who did Tessa meet on her adventure?

_____

2 - What did Tessa learn from helping the old man?

_____

3 - How did Tessa's family react to her adventure?

_____

COLOR ME

Read and color the Letter

ought
I CAN READ

Read the story, and identify and underline all the - ought - words.

The Birthday Bouquet

Once upon a time, there was a little girl named Lily. She thought that she ought to buy a present for her best friend's birthday, but she had nought coins. She sought for a solution and came across a man who wrought beautiful flower bouquets. She begged him to teach her how to make one, and he kindly taught her. She then caught a lovely butterfly to put in the bouquet. When she brought the gift to her friend, she was overwrought with joy. The two friends besought to spend the day together and play. They fought imaginary dragons, drank lemonade, and had a grand time

read and write

Write all the "ought" words you can see in the story			

I CAN READ

Read the sentences and answers the questions: Put a check mark

Lily bought a pretty dress

Ava sought for a solution

He wrought a metal sculpture

Questions

1. What did Lily buy?   a pretty dress ☐   car ☐

2. What was ava looking for?   sought for a solution ☐   answer ☐

Write the correct word beside each scrambled word.

thougth ___	wrougth ___	sougth ___
bougth ___	caugth ___	nougth ___
ougth ___	fougth ___	brougth ___

Make sentences

Thought
_____
_____

Bought
_____
_____

Rules
TRACE AND
COLOR

Trace it:

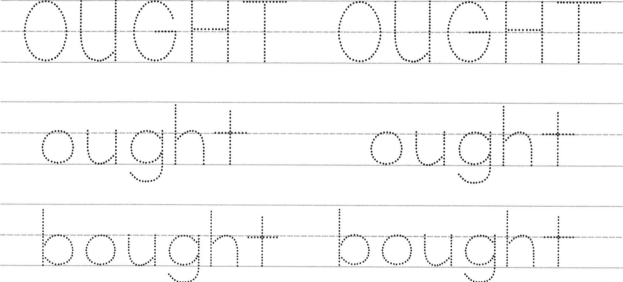

OUGHT OUGHT

ought   ought

bought bought

Colour it:

BOUGHT

I CAN WRITE

Color Me!

Circle the – ought – words

fought   bold   thought

action   sought   bought

nought   tongue   switch

Trace the words

caught

caught

bought

Fill in the missing letters

bough _____ fough _____

though _____ fraugh _____

sought _____ draugh _____

Read and Trace the sentence.

I bought a car

i bought a car

READ AGAIN

Read the story, and answer each question. highlight the answers in the story.

The Birthday Bouquet

Once upon a time, there was a little girl named Lily. She thought that she ought to buy a present for her best friend's birthday, but she had nought coins. She sought for a solution and came across a man who wrought beautiful flower bouquets. She begged him to teach her how to make one, and he kindly taught her. She then caught a lovely butterfly to put in the bouquet. When she brought the gift to her friend, she was overwrought with joy. The two friends besought to spend the day together and play. They fought imaginary dragons, drank lemonade, and had a grand time

Answer Each Question.

1 - Who is the little girl in the story?

_____

2 - Why did Lily want to buy a present?

_____

3 - What did Lily put in the bouquet?

_____

COLOR ME

Read and color the Letter

ought

ph
I CAN READ

Read the story, and identify and underline all the - ph - words.

Phil's Ph Words

Once upon a time, there was a clever elephant named Phil. Phil loved to play games with his friends, but he had trouble pronouncing words with the letter "ph". One day, Phil decided to learn all the words with "ph" and went to the library. He read books and practiced saying words like "phone", "photograph", and "alphabet". With each day, Phil's confidence grew, and he became a master of "ph" words. His friends were amazed by his progress and started using "ph" words too. Now, Phil and his friends played fun games where they only used "ph" words. Phil was happy he had learned something new and shared his knowledge with others.

read and write

Write all the "ph" words you can see in the story			

I CAN READ

Read the sentences and answers the questions: Put a check mark

The elephant felt philosophical about life

Phil's nephew liked to play with the alphabet

Phil and his friends enjoyed physical activities

Questions

1. What did Phil's nephew like to play with? The alphabet ☐ toy ☐

2. How did the elephant feel about life? Philosophical ☐ teacher ☐

Write the correct word beside each scrambled word.

phoen ———	phaes ———	pluhs
grahp ———	phantmo ———	sylhp
alpah ———	phoot ———	nymhp

Make sentences

Phone _____

_____

Graph _____

_____

Rules
TRACE AND COLOR

Trace it:

Ph Ph Ph Ph Ph Ph

ph ph ph ph

photo photo

Colour it:

I CAN WRITE

Color Me!

Circle the – ph – words

tophat	plush	patch
action	scratch	sylph
photo	tongue	sylph

Trace the words

sylph sylph
graph graph
phase phase

Fill in the missing letters

phas	_____	stap	_____
phon	_____	topha	_____
sylp	_____	serap	_____

Read and Trace the sentence.

Phil and his friends

phil and his friends

READ AGAIN

Read the story, and answer each question. highlight the answers in the story.

Phil's Ph Words

Once upon a time, there was a clever elephant named Phil. Phil loved to play games with his friends, but he had trouble pronouncing words with the letter "ph". One day, Phil decided to learn all the words with "ph" and went to the library. He read books and practiced saying words like "phone", "photograph", and "alphabet". With each day, Phil's confidence grew, and he became a master of "ph" words. His friends were amazed by his progress and started using "ph" words too. Now, Phil and his friends played fun games where they only used "ph" words. Phil was happy he had learned something new and shared his knowledge with others.

Answer Each Question.

1 - What did Phil decide to do one day?

_____

2 - What were some of the "ph" words Phil learned?

_____

3 - How did Phil's friends react to his progress in learning "ph" words?

_____

COLOR ME

Read and color the Letter

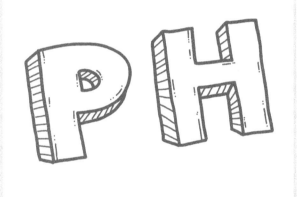

gr
I CAN READ

Read the story, and identify and underline all the - gr - words.

Garden Grill Gathering

Grace and her grandpa loved to garden together. They spent hours planting green grapes and watching them grow. One day, they decided to have a barbeque and invited their friends over. As they were getting the grill ready, Grace tripped and fell, but her grandpa quickly reached out to grasp her and keep her safe. They both smiled and were grateful for each other's company. Soon their friends arrived, and they all formed a group to help prepare the food. They shared stories and laughed together, grateful for the beautiful day and each other's company. As the sun set and they packed up the picnic, Grace hugged her grandpa and grinned. She knew that she was lucky to have such a great grandpa and friends, and that the memories they created that day would last a lifetime.

read and write

Write all the "gr" words you can see in the story			

I CAN READ

Read the sentences and answers the questions: Put a check mark

Jack gave a grateful smile

The grape was juicy

She began to grow

Questions

1. How did Jack express his gratitude? smile ☐ play ☐

2. What was the texture of the grape? juicy ☐ good ☐

Write the correct word beside each scrambled word.

graec _____	grwo _____	graps _____
grene _____	grandap _____	gropu _____
graep _____	grateflu _____	grni _____

Make sentences

Grace _____

_____

Grandpa _____

_____

Rules
TRACE AND
COLOR

Trace it:

GR   GR   GR   GR

gr   gr   gr   gr

green   green

Colour it:

129

I CAN WRITE

Color Me!

great

Circle the - gr - words

great	plush	grill
action	gravel	sylph
grin	tongue	graphic

Trace the words

green green
grow grow
grin grin

Fill in the missing letters

gratefu _____   grea _____

gras _____   gril _____

grou _____   grave _____

Read and Trace the sentence.

The grass is green

The grass is green

130

READ AGAIN

Read the story, and answer each question. highlight the answers in the story.

Garden Grill Gathering

Grace and her grandpa loved to garden together. They spent hours planting green grapes and watching them grow. One day, they decided to have a barbeque and invited their friends over. As they were getting the grill ready, Grace tripped and fell, but her grandpa quickly reached out to grasp her and keep her safe. They both smiled and were grateful for each other's company. Soon their friends arrived, and they all formed a group to help prepare the food. They shared stories and laughed together, grateful for the beautiful day and each other's company. As the sun set and they packed up the picnic, Grace hugged her grandpa and grinned. She knew that she was lucky to have such a great grandpa and friends, and that the memories they created that day would last a lifetime.

Answer Each Question.

1 - Who loved to garden together?

_____

2 - What did Grace and her grandpa plant?

_____

3 - Who helped to prepare the food?

_____

COLOR ME

Read and color the Letter

br
I CAN READ

Read the story, and identify and underline all the - br - words.

Brave Little Benny

There was a brave little bear named Benny who lived in a big brown cave in the middle of the forest. One day, Benny heard a loud noise coming from outside his cave. He peeked his head out and saw a big badger trying to break into his honey stash! Benny knew he had to act fast, so he grabbed his trusty brown backpack and raced outside. He bravely confronted the badger and scared him away, saving his precious honey. Benny returned to his cozy cave, feeling proud of his bravery. From that day on, Benny was known as the bravest bear in the forest.

read and write

Write all the "br" words you can see in the story			

I CAN READ

Read the sentences and answers the questions: Put a check mark

I need a new broom

He took a deep breath

The bridge creaked underfoot

Questions

1. What did he take before speaking?   football ☐   deep breath ☐

2. What household item do you require?   broom ☐   Television ☐

Write the correct word beside each scrambled word.

brave	-----	bronw	-----	brodo	-----
bridge	-----	bruhs	-----	brmi	-----
brigth	-----	breaht	-----	broda	-----

Make sentences

Brave

_____

_____

Brown

_____

_____

Rules
TRACE AND COLOR

Trace it:

BR   BR   BR   BR

br   br   br   br

brood   brood

Colour it:

135

I CAN WRITE

Color Me!

brim

Circle the – br – words

brim	potion	brush
action	breath	option
broad	brunch	stink

Trace the words

brisk

breeze

broccoli

Fill in the missing letters

brav _____   brus _____

bridg _____   broa _____

brow _____   brittl _____

Read and Trace the sentence.

Brave soldier

brave soldier

READ AGAIN

Read the story, and answer each question. highlight the answers in the story.

Brave Little Benny

There was a brave little bear named Benny who lived in a big brown cave in the middle of the forest. One day, Benny heard a loud noise coming from outside his cave. He peeked his head out and saw a big badger trying to break into his honey stash! Benny knew he had to act fast, so he grabbed his trusty brown backpack and raced outside. He bravely confronted the badger and scared him away, saving his precious honey. Benny returned to his cozy cave, feeling proud of his bravery. From that day on, Benny was known as the bravest bear in the forest.

Answer Each Question.

1 - What was the name of the bear in the story?

_____

2 - What did Benny hear outside his cave?

_____

3 - How did Benny scare the badger away?

_____

COLOR ME

Read and color the Letter

pl

I CAN READ

Read the story, and identify and underline all the - pl - words.

Penelope's Kindness

In a land of playful puppies and pretty ponies, lived a little girl named Penelope. Penelope loved to play in the park, especially on the swings and the slide. One day, while playing, she noticed a small bird with a broken wing. She felt sad for the bird and wanted to help. She ran home and grabbed a blanket and some bread crumbs. She carefully picked up the bird and wrapped it in the blanket. She gave it some bread crumbs and stayed with it until it fell asleep. The next day, she took the bird to a veterinarian who fixed its wing. Penelope was happy to see the bird fly away and she knew that she had done something good. The end.

read and write

Write all the "pl" words you can see in the story			

I CAN READ

Read the sentences and answers the questions: Put a check mark

Paula planted pretty purple flowers

The plumber fixed the leaking pipe

The playground was full of playful children

Questions

1. What did Paula plant?   tomato ☐   purple flowers ☐

2. What was the playground full of?   balls ☐   playful children ☐

Write the correct word beside each scrambled word.

platn _____   plaen _____   plukc _____

pladi _____   plakn _____   pluhs _____

plati _____   plaet _____   plante _____

Make sentences

Plenty _____

_____

Plane _____

_____

Rules
TRACE AND COLOR

Trace it:

Pl   Pl   Pl   Pl   Pl

pl   pl   pl   pl

plate   plate

Colour it:

I CAN WRITE

Color Me!

pluck

Circle the – pl – words

pluck	plaid	brush
action	breath	plane
plush	pliable	stink

Trace the words

plank
platter
plumber

Fill in the missing letters

platte ———   plasti ———

plent ———   pluc ———

plum ———   plan ———

Read and Trace the sentence.

Wooden plank plane

wooden plank plane

READ AGAIN

Read the story, and answer each question. highlight the answers in the story.

Penelope's Kindness

In a land of playful puppies and pretty ponies, lived a little girl named Penelope. Penelope loved to play in the park, especially on the swings and the slide. One day, while playing, she noticed a small bird with a broken wing. She felt sad for the bird and wanted to help. She ran home and grabbed a blanket and some bread crumbs. She carefully picked up the bird and wrapped it in the blanket. She gave it some bread crumbs and stayed with it until it fell asleep. The next day, she took the bird to a veterinarian who fixed its wing. Penelope was happy to see the bird fly away and she knew that she had done something good. The end.

Answer Each Question.

1 - Where did Penelope like to play in the park?

_____

2 - What did Penelope notice while she was playing in the park?

_____

3 - What did Penelope do to help the bird?

_____

COLOR ME

Read and color the Letter

bl

I CAN READ

Read the story, and identify and underline all the - bl - words.

Blake's Brave Shark Adventure

Blake was a brave boy who loved to explore the deep blue sea. He dreamt of discovering a new kind of creature that nobody had ever seen before. One day, while diving, he stumbled upon a huge underwater cave. He bravely swam inside, his flashlight illuminating the dark and murky waters. Suddenly, he saw something that made his heart race with excitement – a gigantic black blade! It was unlike anything he had ever seen before. Blake carefully approached it and realized that it was the fin of a massive black shark! He quickly swam away, but he knew that he had just discovered something amazing. Blake couldn't wait to tell his friends about his incredible adventure!

read and write

Write all the "bl" words you can see in the story			

I CAN READ

Read the sentences and answers the questions: Put a check mark

The blue sky was cloudless

The black cat crossed stealthily

Jack used a blunt pencil

Questions

1. What was the condition of the sky?   cloudy ☐   was cloudless ☐
2. How did the black cat cross?   running ☐   stealthily ☐

Write the correct word beside each scrambled word.

bleu _____	blikn _____	blto _____
blakc _____	blutn _____	bluhs _____
blaed _____	blaer _____	blaez _____

Make sentences

Blade
_____
_____

Bliss
_____
_____

Rules
TRACE AND COLOR

Trace it:

BL   BL   BL   BL

bl   bl   bl   bl

blade   blade

Colour it:

147

I CAN WRITE

Color Me!

blunt

Circle the - bl - words

blunt	plaid	blare
blimp	blade	plane
blend	pliable	stink

Trace the words

blink
blabber
blister

Fill in the missing letters

bliste ____   blac ____

blen ____   blu ____

blith ____   blad ____

Read and Trace the sentence.

I have a blue bike

i have a blue bike

READ AGAIN

Read the story, and answer each question. highlight the answers in the story.

Blake's Brave Shark Adventure

Blake was a brave boy who loved to explore the deep blue sea. He dreamt of discovering a new kind of creature that nobody had ever seen before. One day, while diving, he stumbled upon a huge underwater cave. He bravely swam inside, his flashlight illuminating the dark and murky waters. Suddenly, he saw something that made his heart race with excitement – a gigantic black blade! It was unlike anything he had ever seen before. Blake carefully approached it and realized that it was the fin of a massive black shark! He quickly swam away, but he knew that he had just discovered something amazing. Blake couldn't wait to tell his friends about his incredible adventure!

Answer Each Question.

1 - Who is Blake and what is his passion?

_____

2 - What did Blake discover while diving one day?

_____

3 - What did Blake feel when he saw the fin of the black shark?

_____

COLOR ME

Read and color the Letter

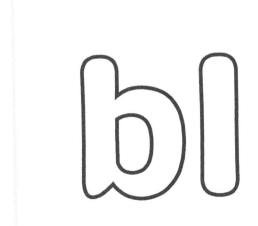

gl
I CAN READ

Read the story, and identify and underline all the - gl - words.

Glen's Glittery Adventure

Glen was a little boy who loved playing outside. One day, while exploring the woods, he came across a glowing lantern. As he picked it up, he felt a strange sensation in his hands. Suddenly, he found himself transported to a magical land where everything was made of glitter and gold. Giant glittery creatures welcomed him, and he knew he had to explore this magical place. As he wandered, he found a golden castle with a princess trapped inside. Glen bravely fought the giant glittery dragon guarding the castle and freed the princess. As they returned to their world, Glen knew he had made a friend for life.

read and write

Write all the "gl" words you can see in the story			

151

I CAN READ

Read the sentences and answers the questions: Put a check mark

Glum faces filled the room

Snow globe shook, creating magical scene

Sun glinted off the ocean waves

Questions

1. What created a magical scene by shaking?   toy ☐ snow globe ☐

2. What glinted off the ocean waves?   sun glinted ☐   car ☐

Write the correct word beside each scrambled word.

glaez _____   gloeb _____   glaed _____

glomo _____   glitn _____   glude _____

glied _____   glaer _____   glota _____

Make sentences

Globe _____

_____

_____

Glove _____

_____

_____

Rules
TRACE AND
COLOR

Trace it:

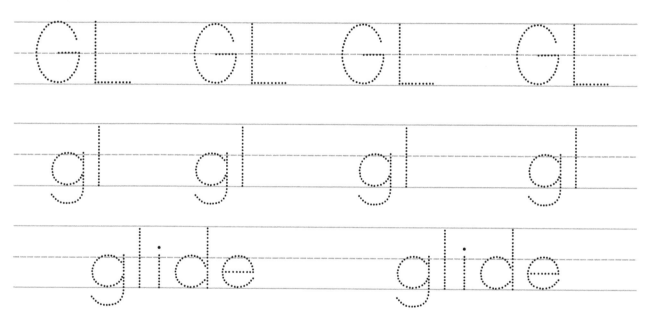

G L   G L   G L   G L

g l   g l   g l   g l

glide   glide

Colour it:

I CAN WRITE

Color Me!

Circle the – gl – words

blunt	glaze	blare
glide	blade	glove
blend	glued	stink

Trace the words

glitz
glory
gloam

Fill in the missing letters

gloa _____   glan _____

glaz _____   glar _____

glue _____   glid _____

Read and Trace the sentence.

Globe in corner

globe in corner

READ AGAIN

Read the story, and answer each question. highlight the answers in the story.

Glen's Glittery Adventure

Glen was a little boy who loved playing outside. One day, while exploring the woods, he came across a glowing lantern. As he picked it up, he felt a strange sensation in his hands. Suddenly, he found himself transported to a magical land where everything was made of glitter and gold. Giant glittery creatures welcomed him, and he knew he had to explore this magical place. As he wandered, he found a golden castle with a princess trapped inside. Glen bravely fought the giant glittery dragon guarding the castle and freed the princess. As they returned to their world, Glen knew he had made a friend for life.

Answer Each Question.

1 - What did Glen do to free the princess?

_____

2 - What did Glen find in the golden castle?

_____

3 - Who welcomed Glen in the magical place?

_____

COLOR ME

Read and color the Letter

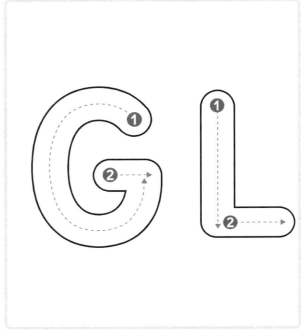

dr
I CAN READ

Read the story, and identify and underline all the - dr - words.

Magical Doctor Daisy

Dr. Daisy was a kind doctor who loved to help kids feel better. She had a magical clinic that was full of toys and games to make her patients feel comfortable. One day, a little girl named Dora came to see Dr. Daisy. Dora had a bad cold and was feeling very sick. Dr. Daisy gave her a check-up and listened to her cough. "Don't worry, Dora," Dr. Daisy said with a smile. "I'm going to give you some medicine that will help you feel better." Dr. Daisy mixed up a special medicine that tasted like strawberries and gave it to Dora. She also gave her a sticker to put on her shirt. "Thank you, Dr. Daisy," Dora said as she left the clinic feeling much better. Dr. Daisy knew that helping kids feel better was the most magical thing of all.

read and write

Write all the "dr" words you can see in the story			

I CAN READ

Read the sentences and answers the questions: Put a check mark

She dreamed of becoming an astronaut

The girl danced in her dress

She drove the car carefully

Questions

1. How did she drive?   carefully ☐   slowly ☐

2. What did she dream?   becoming an astronaut ☐   doctor ☐

Write the correct word beside each scrambled word.

drema _____   driev _____   drosp _____

dritf _____   dranw _____   dritf _____

dreda _____   draep _____   drudi _____

Make sentences

Dream _____

_____

_____

Drawn _____

_____

_____

Rules
TRACE AND COLOR

Trace it:

DR   DR   DR   DR

dr   dr   dr   dr

drone   drone

Colour it:

I CAN WRITE

Color Me!

drupe

Circle the - dr - words

drupe	glaze	dare
glide	drape	glove
druid	drupe	stink

Trace the words

drags
dress
drone

Fill in the missing letters

dron ——— driv ———

dar ——— drif ———

drin ——— drui ———

Read and Trace the sentence.

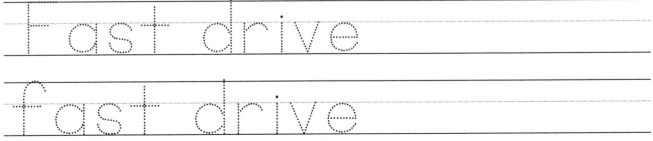

Fast drive

fast drive

READ AGAIN

Read the story, and answer each question. highlight the answers in the story.

Magical Doctor Daisy

Dr. Daisy was a kind doctor who loved to help kids feel better. She had a magical clinic that was full of toys and games to make her patients feel comfortable. One day, a little girl named Dora came to see Dr. Daisy. Dora had a bad cold and was feeling very sick. Dr. Daisy gave her a check-up and listened to her cough. "Don't worry, Dora," Dr. Daisy said with a smile. "I'm going to give you some medicine that will help you feel better." Dr. Daisy mixed up a special medicine that tasted like strawberries and gave it to Dora. She also gave her a sticker to put on her shirt. "Thank you, Dr. Daisy," Dora said as she left the clinic feeling much better. Dr. Daisy knew that helping kids feel better was the most magical thing of all.

Answer Each Question.

1 - Who is Dr. Daisy?

_____

2 - What did Dr. Daisy give Dora?

_____

3 - How did Dora feel after visiting Dr. Daisy's clinic?

_____

COLOR ME

Read and color the Letter

kn
I CAN READ

Read the story, and identify and underline all the - kn - words.

Knox's Flying Machine

Knox was a clever little boy who loved to learn new things. He spent hours reading books and asking questions. One day, Knox's class was given a science project to do. They had to build a machine that could fly. Knox was excited about the project and started researching different types of flying machines. He learned about airplanes, helicopters, and hot air balloons. Knox knew that building a flying machine was not going to be easy, but he was determined to do it. Knox spent weeks working on his project, and finally, the day of the presentation arrived. Knox's machine was not the fanciest, but it flew higher and farther than any of the other machines. Knox was thrilled and proud of himself for all his hard work and knowledge.

read and write

Write all the "kn" words you can see in the story			

I CAN READ

Read the sentences and answers the questions: Put a check mark

He had a knack for fixing cars

He used a knife to cut the bread

The child knelt down to tie his shoes

Questions

1. What did he use the knife for?   to cut the bread ☐   to play ☐

2. What did the child do?   tie his shoes ☐   knock ☐

Write the correct word beside each scrambled word.

knakc _____   knetl _____   knikc _____

knonw _____   kneda _____   knist _____

knief _____   knosb _____   knese _____

Make sentences

Known _____

_____

_____

Knife _____

_____

_____

Trace it:

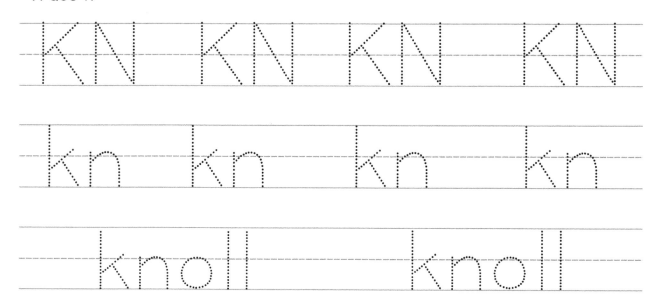

Colour it:

I CAN WRITE

Color Me!

knobs

Circle the - kn - words

knobs	knick	blare
glide	knees	glove
knurl	glued	knoll

Trace the words

known
knife
knead

Fill in the missing letters

knif _____   knav _____

knit _____   knee _____

knee _____   knop _____

Read and Trace the sentence.

I knew that

i knew that

READ AGAIN

Read the story, and answer each question. highlight the answers in the story.

Knox's Flying Machine

Knox was a clever little boy who loved to learn new things. He spent hours reading books and asking questions. One day, Knox's class was given a science project to do. They had to build a machine that could fly. Knox was excited about the project and started researching different types of flying machines. He learned about airplanes, helicopters, and hot air balloons. Knox knew that building a flying machine was not going to be easy, but he was determined to do it. Knox spent weeks working on his project, and finally, the day of the presentation arrived. Knox's machine was not the fanciest, but it flew higher and farther than any of the other machines. Knox was thrilled and proud of himself for all his hard work and knowledge.

Answer Each Question.

1 - What did Knox love to do?

_____

2 - How did Knox feel about the science project?

_____

3 - How did Knox feel after presenting his machine?

_____

COLOR ME

Read and color the Letter

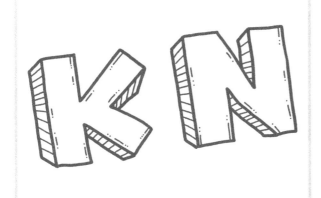

sc

I CAN READ

Read the story, and identify and underline all the - sc - words.

Scary Ocean Adventure

Samantha the Scientist loved to explore the ocean. She built a special submarine that could travel to the deepest parts of the sea. One day, Samantha saw a scary creature with sharp teeth swimming towards her. She quickly scanned it with her scope and realized it was just a friendly seahorse! Samantha was relieved and smiled as she watched the seahorse swim away. Suddenly, she heard a loud screech coming from her submarine's engine. She was scared that it might break down, but then she remembered that she was a scientist and she could fix it. Samantha used her tools to repair the engine and continued her exploration. She saw schools of colorful fish, giant sea turtles, and even a sunken treasure! Samantha realized that even though the ocean could be scary sometimes, it was full of wonders waiting to be discovered.

read and write

Write all the "sc" words you can see in the story			

I CAN READ

Read the sentences and answers the questions: Put a check mark

Tom wore a cozy scarf skiing

Science class was fun and interesting

The scuba diver saw beautiful coral

Questions

1. What did Tom wear while skiing?   cozy scarf ☐   helmit ☐

2. What was science class like?   interesting ☐   good ☐

Write the correct word beside each scrambled word.

scarde _____	scayr _____	scafr _____
scienec _____	scoer _____	scholo
scuab	scoep _____	scolw

Make sentences

School _____
_____
_____

Scale _____
_____
_____

Rules
TRACE AND COLOR

Trace it:

Sc Sc Sc Sc

sc sc sc sc

scarf   scarf

Colour it:

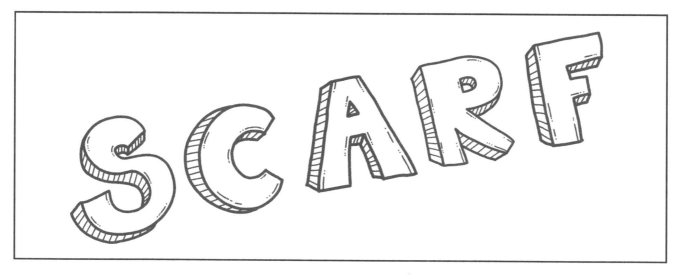

I CAN WRITE

Color Me!

scale

Circle the – sc – words

scale	knick	scurry
glide	scarf	glove
score	glued	knoll

Trace the words

score
scarf
scratch

Fill in the missing letters

scub _____   scratc _____

scar _____   scow _____

schoo _____   scal _____

Read and Trace the sentence.

The scary movie

The scary movie

READ AGAIN

Read the story, and answer each question. highlight the answers in the story.

Scary Ocean Adventure

Samantha the Scientist loved to explore the ocean. She built a special submarine that could travel to the deepest parts of the sea. One day, Samantha saw a scary creature with sharp teeth swimming towards her. She quickly scanned it with her scope and realized it was just a friendly seahorse! Samantha was relieved and smiled as she watched the seahorse swim away. Suddenly, she heard a loud screech coming from her submarine's engine. She was scared that it might break down, but then she remembered that she was a scientist and she could fix it. Samantha used her tools to repair the engine and continued her exploration. She saw schools of colorful fish, giant sea turtles, and even a sunken treasure! Samantha realized that even though the ocean could be scary sometimes, it was full of wonders waiting to be discovered.

Answer Each Question.

1 - What did Samantha build to explore the ocean?

_____

2 - What did Samantha realize about the scary creature?

_____

3 - What did Samantha hear from her submarine's engine?

_____

COLOR ME

Read and color the Letter

sh
I CAN READ

Read the story, and identify and underline all the – sh – words.

Shoreline Treasure Hunt

Samantha and her brother Shawn loved to play by the shore. One day, they found a shiny seashell that led them to a hidden cave. Inside the cave, they discovered a treasure map! Excited about their new discovery, they decided to follow the map to find the treasure. As they walked along the shore, they saw a shadowy shape in the water. They were scared it was a shark, but it turned out to be a friendly dolphin! The dolphin led them to a beautiful lagoon where they found the treasure – a chest filled with shiny shells, colorful pebbles, and a shiny silver coin. Samantha and Shawn were thrilled with their discovery and couldn't wait to show their parents. They realized that sometimes, a little bit of courage can lead to great adventures!

read and write

Write all the "sh" words you can see in the story			

I CAN READ

Read the sentences and answers the questions: Put a check mark

She wore a blue shirt

She took a quick shower

Ava used a shovel to dig

Questions

1. What was she wearing?   blue shirt ☐   helmit ☐

2. What did she do quickly?   quick shower ☐   write ☐

Write the correct word beside each scrambled word.

shpo _____	shrgu _____	shattre _____
shotu _____	showre _____	shadwo _____
shitr _____	shpi _____	shovle _____

Make sentences

Shirt _____

_____

_____

Shop _____

_____

_____

Rules
TRACE AND COLOR

Trace it:

SH SH SH SH SH SH SH

sh sh sh sh

ship ship ship

Colour it:

I CAN WRITE

Color Me!

Shine

Circle the – sh – words

shine	knick	share
glide	sheep	glove
shine	shrug	knoll

Trace the words

shower
shatter
shadow

Fill in the missing letters

shi ——— shir ———

shru ——— shrie ———

shove ——— shallo ———

Read and Trace the sentence.

The shark swam

The shark swam

READ AGAIN

Read the story, and answer each question. highlight the answers in the story.

Shoreline Treasure Hunt

Samantha and her brother Shawn loved to play by the shore. One day, they found a shiny seashell that led them to a hidden cave. Inside the cave, they discovered a treasure map! Excited about their new discovery, they decided to follow the map to find the treasure. As they walked along the shore, they saw a shadowy shape in the water. They were scared it was a shark, but it turned out to be a friendly dolphin! The dolphin led them to a beautiful lagoon where they found the treasure – a chest filled with shiny shells, colorful pebbles, and a shiny silver coin. Samantha and Shawn were thrilled with their discovery and couldn't wait to show their parents. They realized that sometimes, a little bit of courage can lead to great adventures!

Answer Each Question.

1 - What did Samantha and Shawn find in the hidden cave?

_____

2 - What did they find in the lagoon?

_____

3 - What did they think they saw in the water at first?

_____

COLOR ME

Read and color the Letter

THANK YOU

Thank you for choosing this decodable book for your child in second grade. I appreciate your trust in my work and I hope this book will prove to be a valuable tool in your child's reading journey.

As a writer, my goal has always been to create resources that promote reading and make it an enjoyable experience for young readers. This book is designed to help struggling readers improve their decoding skills and gain confidence in their reading abilities.

I have taken a structured approach in this book, teaching children the sounds that letters make in a specific order. I have also included activities in each passage that are designed to reinforce phonemic awareness and promote skill development. My hope is that with the help of this book, your child will build a solid foundation in reading and become a confident and proficient reader in no time.

Once again, thank you for choosing this book. I would love to hear your feedback on this book and how it has helped your child. Your opinion matters to me and it will assist me in creating more valuable resources for young readers in the future.

Thank you for your support and happy reading!

Best regards,

[Jed Dolton]

Printed in the USA
CPSIA information can be obtained
at www.ICGtesting.com
CBHW081348140324
5378CB00017B/1501

9 781960 809063